Neal Rzepkowski, M.D.

Through a Medium's Eyes

Richard Flechsenhaar, "Mountain Man,"
creator of the crewel embroidery in the cover photo.

More by Ruth Shilling

Through a Medium's Eyes Series
About Life, Love, Mediumship, and the Spirit World
Rev. B. Anne Gehman, Volume 1
Carol Gasber, Volume 2
Neal Rzepkowski, M.D., Volume 3
Rev. Simon James, Volume 4
Rev. Brian Robertson, Volume 5

The Egyptian Gods & Goddesses Cards
An original set of cards. See godsgoddessescards.com.

Color It True Series: *Adult Coloring Books that Draw Good Things to You!* Manifestation Mandalas, Volumes 1-5

SUCCESS with the Violin and Life: *Strategies, Techniques and Tips for Learning Quickly and Doing Well.* See successviolin.com.

SINAI: *The Desert and Bedouins of South Sinai's Central Regions.* Palm Press, Cairo, Egypt, 2003

Through a Medium's Eyes

About Life, Love, Mediumship, and the Spirit World

Neal Rzepkowski, M.D.

Volume 3

Through a Medium's Eyes Series

RUTH SHILLING

All One World Books & Media

ISBN : 978-1-945963-03-2

Published by All One World Books & Media
West Kingston, RI, USA • all1world.com

I dedicate this book to

Rev. Penny Donovan (Thorne).

"We are *infinite.*"

Neal Rzepkowski

I dedicate this book to

my mom, Carolyn Whitmore Shilling,

and to all those in the spirit world

who love and inspire us.

Ruth Shilling

Table of Contents

◆◆◆◆◆◆◆◆◆◆◆◆

Introduction

Story: Really?!

My mother passed to the spirit world in 2013. I own and operate a tour business and was just about to leave the country for five weeks of tours in Egypt. With a slight delay for the funeral and legal arrangements, I landed in Cairo to begin leading our tours of the ancient sacred sites.

As I awoke each morning I felt my mom there with me, wishing me well on my day. Really?! It was the same gentle support and encouragement I had felt when with her in the past, but now here she *was* ("Is this possible?" I thought) right there in my hotel room in Cairo, and in my cabin on the cruise boat, and later in Luxor....

This was new for me. It was very clear it was my mom. But there was no physicality to it, just a feeling like I would have had if my eyes were closed and she was there in the room with me. I would *know* she was there. And there were words of supportive encouragement "sounding" in my head, too, a bit like remembering something someone said to me.

These visits were warm and embracing, and certainly left me feeling loved and supported, but I still felt grief about her having gone. However, it did open me up to a new possibility, the idea that our relationship *would* continue, though in a new and different way.

When I returned to the U.S., I got very interested in mediumship: what it is, how it works, who can do it ... I had lots of questions.

Twenty years earlier I had visited the Lily Dale Assembly in western New York and taught classes there in sound healing. Through doing healing and spiritual growth work, I had developed a vibrant and working relationship with the wonderful loving guidance that is our birthright.

At first I thought the source of this helpful guidance was the Holy Spirit but, as it often felt that it was a group that was helping me, I later described it as angels, guides, or just "the helpers." Once in a while, as I was doing a healing session, this guidance would take the form of someone's deceased mother or father, but I never really gave that much thought.

The relationship I *was* aware of was with a pool of loving, wise guides/healers/teachers who helped me both in my own life's struggles and in the healing, guidance, and teaching that I did to serve others.

It never occurred to me that some of this help I was receiving might be from my own grandparents or other people I knew who had died.

But now, after having had these experiences of my mom showing up, it was time to investigate this whole strata of spirit world communication, what I now know is called "contact with deceased loved ones." In other words, not just guides and angels, but everyday *people* who have died.

Where to go to find out? Lily Dale, of course! Mediumship is the core of the Lily Dale Assembly community. For more than a century, mediums there have been making contact with people who have passed to the world of spirit but still have loved ones here who wish to contact them.

Thus started my education and training in this wonderful world of possibility with spirit people (and animals!) who continue to love us and care about our well-being, even in their now less-physical state.

The teachers of these many classes were extraordinary people (in the truest sense of the word, definitely beyond the ordinary) with fascinating experiences I had never even thought of. Certainly not what we might normally hear or read about in the media. To them the spirit world was not *out there* or *up there*, but right *here*, right now!

I kept remarking to myself that these very special people had so much to offer the rest of us – to open our perspectives, widen our beliefs, refresh our ideas. However, many of the mediums were not interested in keeping abreast with the new technology and did not have blogs, websites or books. That meant only a few of us got to hear their stories and perspectives.

BING!!

Through a Medium's Eyes Series
About Life, Love, Mediumship, and the Spirit World

The light goes on, and an idea is born to create a series of short books that share with the rest of us these mediums' unique and wonderful perspectives of the nonphysical world, as well as how that wider vision has informed their own philosophies, beliefs, and understandings about this world we live in.

And so this series of books was born.

Hopefully you will find them both interesting and expanding of your own world and vision.

Ruth Shilling

CHAPTER ONE

Who is Neal Rzepkowski?

Story: From Fear and Condemnation into Peace

Neal: Louis was a very angry man who had AIDS. It was around 1985-86. AZT was not out yet, so he was basically "AIDS wasting," (where you just get weaker and weaker, and then off into the sunset...). He got too weak for office visits, so I would go and do home visits for him. His lover had left him. He had alienated everybody — all his friends — and his family didn't want much to do with him, so I got visiting nurses to come in and care for him.

On one of these home visits, we talked a little bit, and he said, "Well, I am afraid to die. I have alienated everybody, so I know I am going to hell."

"Oh. Is that your belief?"

"Yes, I know I am going to hell."

I said, "Well, I don't believe in hell."

"Why not tell me about your beliefs?"

"In my belief system, when you are going to die, you don't go to hell."

"Well, what happens?"

"You'll be at peace when you die, and normally there is somebody that you knew that will help you over. Is there anybody in your family who you actually *liked*?"

He said, "Well... yes. My grandmother. She was the only one I could get along with. We had a special relationship."

"So don't be surprised if a few days before your death, because you are so nervous about going, your grandma's going to come here. You might think you are hallucinating, but she may come here and prepare you to go. And you are going to go in a peaceful way if you see your grandma. So don't be afraid if you see her."

A few months later I am doing a home visit for him, and he says quite matter-of-factly to me, "Well, tonight I'm going to die."

I said, "Really? Why do you think that?"

"Remember that talk we had a few months ago?"

"Yes."

"I saw my grandmother three days ago and she said she is coming for me tonight. I am okay. Thank you for sharing what you did. I would have thought it was crazy, but you had told me."

He looked pretty good, not like he would die that night. But I believed him, so I just said, "Oh, that's very interesting."

I went home. Two o'clock in the morning I get a call from the visiting nurse. He had passed and I needed to sign the death certificate.

So Spiritualism helped someone from being afraid to die to instead, passing peacefully into death. Fear into peace.

CATHOLIC PRAYERS

Neal Rzepkowski was born October 3, 1951 in Dunkirk, NY, the oldest in a Catholic family with four children. There was Mass every morning before attending Catholic grade school.

Neal: At that age, I thought God lived in the church and would listen to our prayers in the church. I was in the habit of going to Mass in the morning, but the nuns also encouraged us to stop by church in the afternoon to pray. So on the way home, once in a while I would go to pray, which (looking back now) was really like meditating.

As I got a little older, I realized I was gay and that was a mortal sin, so I used to go and say thousands of rosaries that I wouldn't turn out that way. I condemned myself for it and felt inferior.

Ruth: Did you think that God held that against you?

Neal: Well, that's what I was told. Those kinds of feelings were wrong. And I would think, why did God do that to me?

In the 7th or 8th grade we had these sex talks at school, and the priest said that some boys like boys, but they grow out of it as they get older. So I would go to church a lot and pray about it, that I would grow out of it.

Ruth: So that really affected your relationship with the Divine.

Neal: Absolutely. So I became kind of sensitive. I wasn't psychic or anything (that I was aware of), but I was praying all the time from an early age.

My senior year in high school I was an exchange student in France, and I loved to go in the cathedrals to pray and meditate there.

Ruth: So even though you had the feeling that there was "something wrong with you" and God wouldn't be happy with you, you still were having positive experiences through the church? You felt some sort of solace there or something?

Neal: I did. After I got back from France I had an epiphany. After all this praying, all these rosaries, all this guilt (even though I had never acted on my feelings), and all this stuff, I was in the parking lot of the Dunkirk Fredonia Thruway Plaza, and on the radio came the Beatles singing, "Let it be. Mother Mary comes to me, let it be..." I'd been praying to Mother Mary for ages! That was the answer to my prayer after all those years.

Let it be. Just go with the flow. Let it be. I just broke down in tears and started to self-accept.

FIRST VISIT TO LILY DALE ASSEMBLY

The Lily Dale Assembly is a spiritualist community in western New York. There are some 50+ mediums who live and serve there. Registered mediums give readings in their homes to the many visitors, especially during the summer months when the community hosts many interesting speakers, and offers a daily schedule of message services, healing services, and workshops. *See page 90 for info.*

Neal: During high school, before I went to France, I came to Lily Dale. I was working at a YMCA summer camp and on counselors' night out, the closest place to come was Lily Dale. Back in those days, there was no gate fee after 6 p.m. There was an evening Thought Exchange, so I got exposed to Spiritualist philosophy. I also went to "The Stump" and saw some of the outdoor message services, so I got interested in it.

That first summer I had my first reading ever. Five bucks, a high school special. The medium was Tom Bartlett (long gone now). He brought through my Uncle Frank. By name, by description, and everything. I could verify that he was talking to my Uncle Frank. He also gave some predictions — which I had no way of proving — one of which was that I would become a doctor.

I thought, "If this is really so with my Uncle Frank, there is an afterlife. Whether there are angels or not, it proves there is something beyond the physical that's real, something that can be reached. And, if my Uncle Frank — who was no saint — could come and speak to me from the spirit world, and this guy — who was no Catholic — was giving him to me, then I should be able to do it, too." I thought, "He's a human being, I'm a human being. If he can do it, I can do it, too, so long as I am interested enough."

The only way I could believe it is if I could do it or... if I can't, there's a trick. If it is a trick, I am going to stick to it until I find out what it is.

INVESTIGATING SPIRITUALISM

During his college years, Neal took development classes at a Spiritualist church in Albany, NY. It was here that he met his longtime friend and mentor, Rev. Penny Donovan.

Neal: Penny was the pastor of the church and a wonderful medium. I didn't know what it was, but when I watched her talk, there was this yellow light around her. I thought, "That's a halo! She's a saint!"

See page 51 for more about Neal's first spiritual development classes and how he discovered "the trick."

After years of working in development classes, Neal was able to achieve the skill of mediumship. He has now been a registered medium at the Lily Dale Assembly for 34 years and in 2017 became Lily Dale's president.

Story: A Desire for New Property was Fulfilled

For a number of years Neal lived on Buffalo Street in the Dale, but later moved to some property nearby where he could have a garden and also host a number of other activities.

Ruth: So you told Spirit you felt kind of restricted in the Dale itself...

Neal: I said, "Wouldn't it be nice if I had some land where I could have a garden, maybe about 10-20 acres, within a five mile radius of Lily Dale, for $8,000 or less (because that's all the cash that I have)." That was in November 1988, and within two weeks, I got this land at a tax auction for $8,000. There was a rundown hunting cabin on it and it was 13 acres. I also wanted a little creek running through it, and it's got a beaver pond on the corner of it with a creek that runs through it.

Ruth: Now when you did that, were you already familiar with manifestation and how that works? Or did you do that without really realizing?

Neal: I put this out to the universe that I would like to have it, but not that I *had to* have it. And that I would use it for other things with people. At the time I didn't know what, but I felt garden, back to the land, that kind of thing.

Ruth: So at that point you had enough awareness that articulating it would be helpful, but you also knew not to hold onto it. It was articulating, "this is what I would really like," and then letting it go. Is that correct?

Neal: Yes, and then thinking that in the back of my mind I am going to be conscious of opportunities where this may come about. And then within just a couple weeks there was the tax auction. So I thought, "Oh, maybe there is something. I'll look around Lily Dale." This property was up and when I saw it, I thought, "This would be good." I didn't envision a house. I just wanted a garden and some land for time to be away from Lily Dale.

I happened to learn about Native American sweat lodge and ceremony about a year after I got the land. So I thought, "I have this land. I can put a lodge on it," (spirit actually told me to do it and gave me signs about that). *See page 16 for a story about how Neal received the signs that helped him do the sweat lodge ceremonies.*

So I was doing sweat lodges and teaching some people to do sweat lodge. Bob and Steve were really into it and starting to do their own. I was pouring at a sweat lodge for them one day and I got a download from Spirit. It was the oddest thing. I said, "I see you both dancing in a sun dance."

Neal and his father built his home (a geodesic dome)
on some wooded property near Lily Dale.

Beautiful woodwork on a wall on the bedroom loft
is decorated with gifts from friends.

I had been involved in a couple sun dances just to go and support.

"Oh, no, we'll never dance in a sun dance. That's for the Indians. You know, we're white guys."

"Well, this is what I got and just had to share it with you. Have you ever been to a sun dance?"

"Well, no, but that's for them."

"You might be interested to go with me. They have lodges and the sun dance in Pennsylvania."

"Okay, we'll come next year."

So they go to support. Like I did, they are there watching. The next thing I know, the next year they are sun dancing!

Soon Bob and Steve started encouraging Neal to do it, too, but he didn't feel inspired by spirit to do that.

They were pestering me about doing the sun dance, and I said, "You know it's odd that you say I should sun dance, because I feel I am very intimately involved in the sun dance, but I am not dancing."

And now I have the sun dance here on my land! Every year for the last four years!

The site of the Sundance Ceremonies on Neal's property.

CHAPTER TWO

Prayer
&
Meditation

Ruth: What do you recommend as ways to access wise and loving guidance?

Neal: Prayer and meditation. There is a passage in the bible that says, "Seek and ye shall find. Knock and it shall be opened." The translation the way I say it is, "Persist in knocking and eventually you'll get it. Be persistent in seeking and eventually you will find."

Edgar Cayce also said that you need to be **persistent and consistent** in order to get the guidance you seek.

Expectation. Be expectant that it will come, but without regimentation. It may come in a different way than what you expect. It may come from a place that you wouldn't think, or indirectly where you have to connect the dots.

PRAYER

- Be persistent and consistent in asking.
- Be expectant that it will come.
- Be flexible. It may not come in a way that you anticipate.

Ruth: Now when you say "prayer," what exactly do you mean? What's an example?

Neal: You supplicate. "Spirit, I'm in a bad place. Help me out. Give me some inspiration. Give me some guidance. Send something to me."

Ruth: So just to clarify, for you, prayer is where you are requesting things from the Divine?

Neal: Yes. "So look, I have these needs, Divine Order Spirits, spirit helpers."

Ruth: So it's an asking, a supplication. What are your recommendations on meditation?

MEDITATIONS

1. Focus on an object.
2. Focus on the breath.
3. Repeat a mantra.

Neal: There are many types of meditation, and I used to meditate regularly, which I don't now. I try to every night, but for a purpose. I've tried floating; I tried visualization, astral projection, all of which calms down the body and focuses the mind.

Ruth: So you would say that meditation calms down the body and focuses the mind?

Neal: Right. You can focus on a flower and see that flower for 15 minutes straight. Keep bringing your thoughts back to the flower, bring them back to the flower...

You can focus on your breathing. And of course, your mind will wander. Bring your thoughts back to the breathing...

Another thing you can do is say a phrase or a mantra. My favorite one when I am meditating (and I vary it) is, "Peace. Be still and know that I am God."

Peace. Be still and know that I am God.
Peace. Be still and know that I am.
Peace. Be still and know.
Peace. Be still.
Peace. Be.
Peace. Peace. Peace.
(Then backwards)
Peace. Be.
Peace. Be still.
Peace. Be still and know.
Peace. Be still and know that I am.
Peace. Be still and know that I am God.

After doing that once or twice, the meditation time is done. It's just the calming.

Ruth: Why do you think it is good for people to meditate?

Neal: First of all, on a subtle, unconscious level, you are attuning yourself more to your spiritual higher self, and the helpers of your higher self (your guides), and the Divine.

If you are looking to develop mediumship, it helps with that. It helps your anxiety, lowers blood pressure, has health benefits.

There are studies on Transcendental Meditation. Herbert Benson was a Harvard Researcher that found a method he called the Relaxation Response. It is scientifically researched meditation. You don't need a mantra, you can just say the word *one*, which I actually think is a very significant mantra.

Story: "I need a concrete, physical sign."

Neal: In September of 1989 I went with Penny, my spiritual mentor to Bear Butte, the sacred mountain of the Lakota and Cheyenne Indians, north of Rapid City, South Dakota. I had been a medium for 20 years at that point. We asked a park ranger at Bear Butte if we could stay on the ceremonial grounds which is set aside in the state park for Native Americans. She said, nobody is down there, go ahead and camp there. We arc going to close up at the end of September anyway, so it is quiet.

So we went there, set up our camp, just got settled, and at 9:30 at night, here comes a rickety "res-mobile." They are making fires, and I said to Penny, "We'll never get any sleep, so let's go join them."

So we went and they said, "We're making a sweat lodge, come join us." So that was my first sweat lodge ceremony.

Afterwards, that night I couldn't sleep. Spirit came to me and said, "Okay, you did a sweat lodge. Now you do one."

I said, "I can't. I don't have someone to mentor me or teach me, so how am I going to learn this? I didn't get the name of that medicine man to learn how to do these things. They were singing beautiful songs, I didn't get those..."

"We'll teach you."

"Aaaach... this is beyond me."

"Well, we will get you three books."

"Three of them? You mean there are books on this stuff?"

On our last day, on our way to the airport, we stopped at the Sioux trading post which had a bookstore as part of it. Three books practically fell off the shelf!

So Spirit had said, "Do the sweat lodges," but I still thought, "I don't know about this. It must be my ego telling me to do this because I'm an Indian wannabee. I don't have a drop of Indian blood in me so why in the heck would I be getting spirit guides to help me do a sweat lodge?"

I am arguing in my head, so finally I said to them, "You gave me the three books, but why not use an Indian?"

"Well, you're here and there is not enough time," is what they said.

"Alright. If you are really giving me this guidance, I need a concrete, physical sign." I was thinking if I did it on my newly acquired land near Lily Dale, where would I put it? Two owl feathers showed up, right where I would envision the fire pit. "OK. Great horned owl feathers. Very impressive. This might be a message from spirit (feathers are often a message from spirit).

For the Crow Indians the owl is a negative *not-do* sign, so I said to myself, it's really my ego, but I kind of thought they wanted me to do this, so I said, "I need another physical sign."

The next day, *exactly* in the same spot, a hawk feather. But I thought, maybe three is the charm (like Jason's fleece that he sent out).

As I was thinking this, I was looking to the west and someone clairaudiently practically shouts in my head (*in a deep voice*), "Don't push us!" I said, "Alright, alright, alright." *(laughter)*

So I get the sweat lodge built according to the book that fell off the shelf. I am getting ready that very day. I made up some songs because I didn't have the Lakota songs. When I was in the only sweat lodge I ever did, they had a wing that they fanned with.

So I'm arguing with Spirit. "This really is my ego. They had a wing. I don't have a wing. I don't think this is a good idea. I'm a 'Pollack,' rather than a Lakota." I am thinking this as I am driving and a blue jay flew out of a corn field and I hit it. I felt so bad. I get out of the car. The poor blue jay. It's dead.

Symbolically, the number four is very significant for the Native Americans. As I get the blue jay, there are four kernels of corn in its mouth.

They said, "Feed these people. And there's your wing." So I had the wing on the way to the lodge.

Later on I thought, "I need an abalone shell for smudging." I was driving down a road that is usually deserted, but on this day there were people there having a yard sale. There was a huge abalone shell there for $1! "Okay, okay, I got the message."

So there is guidance, and it can come in those confirming coincidental synchronistic events and at the very last minute. You trust and it falls into place. It's amazing stuff.

INSPIRATION & UPLIFTMENT

Neal: What inspires me in mediumship is to watch excellent mediums through their work give healing to an audience. Not only the person they are reading for, but to give healing, evidence, ah-ha, and insight into the spiritual world—that there is something more than what they are doing, they can reach higher.

To watch a good speaker speak on a subject is inspiring. That's where I get personal inspiration, by watching these. When I need inspiration for my sermons, I look at my own life and what I have learned, and I turn to these books.
See page 85, Neal's recommended books.

Ruth: What uplifts you?

Neal: I would either do or go to a sweat lodge ceremony. I would go hiking in the mountains, or camping. I would go polka dancing or country and western line dancing. I love that! Energizing music will uplift me.

◆◆◆◆◆◆◆◆◆◆◆◆

CHAPTER THREE

Teachers
&
Guides

Ruth: What qualities do you value most in a teacher?

GOOD TEACHERS

- Flexible, open minded, nonjudgmental, accepting of differences.
- Willing to explain what their reasons are and be ready to give the reasons for their point of view.
- Continuing to learn and grow themselves, and then sharing what they are learning with their students.
- Model for the students what they want to teach, set the example by being and doing what they want to teach. They embody what they teach.
- Spirit guides never command you. They suggest.

Neal: By *open mindedness* I mean ready to consider other options that are different than what they teach. Nonjudgmental, or judgement in a positive way. Acceptance of differences. They can say, "Here is why I would say..." and give the reasons. Not just, "You should do it this way."

Any good instructor in spiritual ways, including your guides, will never command you. The guides will say, this is a suggestion. Teachers might say, this is the way it works for us, but it is not the only way that is good.

A good teacher continues to learn, and then shares what they are learning with their students.

Ruth: What qualities or attitudes do you try to embody while you are teaching?

Neal: Let's take mediumship as an example. If I am teaching something, I will demonstrate it *before* I teach it. And then I say, here is how it works, and go through step by step the nitty gritty of *how* I am doing it, *what* I am doing, and what I am demonstrating.

That then serves, number one, as a model. Number two, that I'm not just blowing smoke, that I can do this, and therefore, if I can do it, they can do it.

I don't expect anyone to do anything that I can't do, and I certainly can't teach it if I don't know it and cannot do it myself.

Now I am talking about mediumship here (which is a skill). I was also a national educator and speaker on HIV, both to lay and professional audiences. A teacher can read their audience and bring it down to a level that is interesting and understandable to that audience.

MENTORS

Ruth: What advice would you give to someone for choosing a mentor?

Neal: By their fruits you shall know them. So be sure that they walk their talk. There should be some sort of quality in them that you admire and want to emulate, and you want to know something more in depth. Then either ask them if they would be a formal mentor to you, or just put yourself in their presence where you can absorb their knowledge.

I have never asked anyone to be my mentor, but I would say that Penny Donovan, my first spiritual teacher, was like a mentor. She became a friend and a confidant, but in a way she was certainly a mentor and role model.

Rev. Penny Donovan (Thorne)

Ruth: What did she do or say or represent that was helpful to you as a teacher?

Neal: Generally encouraging, nonjudgmental, very loving, very open. I divulged to her that I was homosexual. She was fine with that. "That's the way God made you." No condemnation at all, which was very reassuring.

Ruth: What was spirituality to her?

Neal: I think it was realizing the grandeur, the omnipresence, the vast inexplicable beauty of the divine in everything, and taking joy in it. Realizing how much greater we are than we ever realize. I remember when we were driving somewhere in South Dakota and she said, "We are *infinite*." It came from the depths of her. We are *infinite*, much more than we realize. She was amazed by that.

SPIRIT GUIDES

Ruth: What's your advice to people for making contact with their spirit guides or angels or...?

Neal: Visualization, in either a meditation or a guided visualization, is a way to make contact. You relax yourself and you visualize a guide, a person, or a helpful force coming close to you. There are a lot of guided meditations, "How to meet your guides," that are available now.

Ruth: Who are some of your guides, and how did you meet them?

Neal: As far as spirit guides go, for the first 20 years that I was a medium, I knew I had spirit guides, but I had little idea of who they were. I just knew that they were there. I still have no idea who most of them are, although I am getting some ideas, but they haven't confirmed yet.

However, when I was still in medical school – as a third-year medical student – I was attending a weekly home circle. Occasionally, the leader of the circle would go into trance and bring through information from spirits. I found it intriguing. Then on occasion, another guy in the group started going into trance as well.

One day, I found myself with a voice in my head that was shouting so loud I just had to let go and express it. When I did, I found it was what is called *trance control*. I was conscious of what was happening, but I didn't edit it, didn't plan it. I was sitting there, realizing this stuff was coming out, and listening to it, thinking, "What is this?"

At the time that this happened, I was on a psych rotation in medical school, so I thought, "This is schizophrenia!" But in a way, I realized, this is what trance control is. Not some totally unconscious trance, but trance control. When I would come out of it (as it continued to happen), it would feel like I had been dreaming. Sort of like when you come out of a dream and have to be reminded about snippets of the dream.

Ruth: Was it a positive experience for you?

Neal: It was intriguing. It was nice to know that spirit was working that well through me. I doubted it at first. I thought, "This is my subconscious... this is the wannabee stuff. Maybe this is an aspect of me..." I needed some kind of evidence that this was more than me. Occasionally, he would come out with some things that were happening that I didn't know about (that I learned later were so). So to me that showed he was an independent intelligence that was speaking through me in some way.

Occasionally, he used to come through in classes that I was teaching to do a lesson in trance.

Ruth: How did you know he was there and wanted to talk?

Neal: I would feel a presence behind me of a large male, and I got to know by vibrational feeling that it was Hoho. Or he would be asked to come in.

Ruth: How did you know his name was Hoho?

Neal: We asked him to come in and we asked him his name. He said, "I am not going to give you a name." He was always jovial, laughing and joking with people. He said, "You could call me John. I have been through many lifetimes with different names. I'm not going to give you a name."

Because he was so jovial, it reminded us of Santa Claus and how he would say, "Ho-ho-ho!" So *we* started to call him Hoho. We made up the name. He never said his name, and he still doesn't.

He is a large male Native American, who super-imposes himself. He says he comes through in that persona because he knew me when I lived on the western shore of Lake Michigan. It was a lifetime when we overlapped, so he takes that persona on, even though he said he was also reincarnated in Babylonia and other areas.

He came through for 1-2 years, and very occasionally other spirits would come in. There was one particular one who came in and was very different than Hoho, very soft, and holds my hands very tightly together. He said, "You may call me Lin Chiu." He says my hands are held tightly like that to hold me in a trance state. He says if I was more relaxed, I would lose the connection.

He also said he knew me, but when I was a female in Manchuria in the 1500's. I died of a uterine hemorrhage at that time, and he was my doctor. So we made the connection there.

The interesting thing is, he is more than a person. He is a spokesperson or mouthpiece for a *council* of spirit guides. They can change, depending on the group I am speaking to or the group I am teaching. If I am teaching a group of people, they all have spirit guides. The spirit guides consult to teach the group, and Lin Chiu is the spokesperson for them. He appears to be an individual, but is actually a collective consciousness from the group guides. His accent and his way of teaching varies from class to class because the "committee" changes.

I want to emphasize, this is trance channeling or *trance control*. It is not *deep trance* where I am totally unconscious about what is coming through. I am aware of it on some level.

Ruth: What would you say have been some of the valuable teachings that have come from either Hoho or Lin Chiu?

Neal: Not to take life so seriously. To realize that we are just one little flash-in-the-pan expression in eternity. To realize our thoughts are things. As we have a certain attitude or certain way of thinking, we will create the conditions to make us "correct" in doing that. Everyone loves to be right, so you create your own reality, in a way. It may not be *the truth*, but for you it is. There are different ways to look at things. Also, not to limit ourselves. We look at everything through our time-tinted glasses. We're on a linear time frame in this life, but it's not so because we are having many lives all at once. We also tend to limit our spirit guides to human characteristics and time.

Hoho said, yes he is my guide, but he is not *my* guide. He guides a lot of people. He said, "I am here to guide anybody. If you ask me, I will come to you. Neal doesn't own me. I'll help you, too. Don't be afraid to ask." He has tranced through other people. You can tell it's his personality – not exactly the same as he expresses through me. He also said, "I can be in two places at once. You guys limit me to the physical stuff. No, I can be here and there at the same time." He jokes about it.

Ruth: Do either of them talk about people's specific challenges in life, or is it more the philosophy?

Neal: It's more the philosophy. They specifically shy away from individual readings. They occasionally do it, but they say, "We'll do this this time, but the purpose of us is not for that. It is to teach philosophy." That's their purpose.

Ruth: What do you think their basic agenda is – why they want to come and communicate?

Neal: Lin Chiu's agenda is to facilitate a communication between spirit guides and those on the physical. In so doing, he is also providing a service which is helping his own evolution – because he is serving.

Ruth: With the individuals in the group, he is hoping that what he brings will help them to connect with their own guides?

Neal: Exactly. And in doing that service of being spokesperson for the council he is bringing their guides in so that the people hear what their guides have to teach.

Hoho has several reasons to come through. One is karmic, because he killed me in that lifetime that he knew me. He was jealous of me as a medicine man. He was one also, and he thought he could maybe get what I had by killing me. He realized it didn't work. We're friends now, of course. So he comes kind of as a favor that is owed to me for killing me.

There is an old saying, "We teach best what we need to learn most." So he comes for his own learning and experience. He is also on a path of evolution. He says, "I don't know everything. I am learning myself. I am doing a service and by that I am learning."

◆◆◆◆◆◆◆◆◆◆◆◆

CHAPTER FOUR

The Spirit World

PEOPLE in the SPIRIT WORLD

Ruth: How much are the people in spirit aware of us and our lives? Are they around us 24/7 or... ?

Neal: I think they *can* be around us 24/7, just like your cell phone is around you 24/7. When you think of someone, you can contact them 24/7. That doesn't mean that in every waking moment they are watching you, but they can be *accessed* 24/7, just like your cell phone can access somebody.

It works two ways, too. I think that they can access you and you can access them. They are drawn to you sometimes when you have a thought of them. It's like dialing them in. Or they may have a thought of you, and you suddenly think of them in your mind.

Certainly in times of stress or a need, they will feel that (because of the bonds of love they had in the past when they were on the earth plane with you).

They may be getting a signal that you need help or support, so they will be around you. Of course, if you also ask them, it just amplifies it.

So 24/7 availability, yes, but not constant surveillance. They certainly don't follow you into the bathroom or go into your personal affairs. Even if they did, judgment is suspended upon that vibration in many ways. So I don't think they are there to condemn you, or even to praise you. I think **they are there to help you.**

Ruth: Do they know what we are thinking?

Neal: They have an insight into that. I think in the spirit world, the ones who are attracted to us by the law of vibration have to "lower their vibration" in order to communicate. In so doing, there may not be a clarity with the details of what we are thinking, but they get the general idea. I don't think they are mind readers, any more than they were on the earth plane. I don't think they are privy to every thought in our mind. I think the Absolute Divine is.

They are on a continuing path of evolution, so they may better understand some of the thoughts we have and suspend judgment on those. So I think they pick up our thoughts, just like we pick up their thoughts (and their love and other emotions), but I don't think they necessarily know the absolute detail and clarity of the thoughts.

WHAT HAPPENS WHEN WE DIE

Neal: I think part of what happens when we die is that our expectations, in some way, are met. Those of us who are Christians will meet a Christian figure, Jesus. The Buddhists may meet Buddha. So I think it is an individual experience, rather than a universal one.

If you look at near-death experiences, the descriptions are not one-size-fits-all. You can see some of the person's cultural background in the descriptions of the near-death experience. There are some universal things. For instance, an overwhelming feeling of love, an awareness of a hard-to-explain "Is-ness."

So I think there are some universals in that, but that it is individual, depending upon our cultural training. And who knows, it may even depend upon our past-life experiences. Since there really is no linear time in the world of spirit, we might have some future influences in our passing over into spirit.

Ruth: Do people's personalities change when they are in the spirit world?

Neal: As we continue to evolve in the spirit world, we certainly don't *look* like we did when we were old and decrepit and passing into spirit. We want to look young when we are coming back.

But in a mediumship reading, the spirit is going to identify as you remember them. Often they will come through and give a description of their death – they lost weight, they didn't look good – but then they will say, "But that's over." Then they will appear radiant and young. They want to be seen that way.

So appearances don't follow you into the spirit world. You continue to evolve. But unless they come back in the memory or the *disguise* of what they looked like in the physical (the way the person the reading is for remembers them), you are not going to recognize them.

In my understanding, the Divine Is-ness puts individual "strings" out from the All-That-Is, and those are the divine energies. Those energies, or "soul energies," create an individualization of the All-That-Is.

So the All-That-Is becomes individualized in certain facets, just like how a diamond can have a thousand facets. So an individualized facet is like a soul.

The soul wants to experience many things, including life in the physical. Part of the soul will then project into the physical in a lifetime as a certain personality. That personality is needed in order to have that physical experience.

When the individual with that personality and physical body dies, that personality goes on to the spirit world as recognizable by loved ones who have been here, but the personality is refined and changes, depending upon the soul's other needs – in other lifetimes and in other expressions and in its evolution into the spirit, toward the All-That-Is.

So personalities are kept for identification purposes, but they are not fixed.

We see this almost daily at the outdoor services at Lily Dale. For instance, a medium will bring through a father, and they will say the father was drinking, the father was impulsive, abusive... and now the father comes in to apologize, because his personality, his awareness, has changed in the spirit world. He realizes how awful he was and comes to apologize in a loving way (which does not compute with some of the people who used to know their father), but it is evidence that the personality has evolved.

Story: Is my grandfather my nephew?

I was bringing through a grandfather of a woman I was reading for. I felt his personality traits; I felt the grandfather right there talking to me and describing how he was. At the end of a reading, I like to ask if they have any questions. She asked me, "Is the grandfather reincarnated as my nephew?"

I was thinking, if the grandfather is right here talking to me, how can he be reincarnated as the nephew? But nevertheless, I was tuned in with him so I asked him. He said, "Yes, I am." I thought, "What?! How can you be here talking to me in spirit and say yes, you are incarnated as the nephew?"

He said, "May I remind you that time is only a perception that we have in the physical world. There is no such thing as time over here. My soul is in two places, and it is expressing in the same family line now as the nephew." I told the woman that the grandfather said, yes, and she said, "I thought so! He's got the personality characteristics and the quirks that Grandpa had." Slightly different, but nevertheless, you can identify commonalities in there.

That totally blew me away because I never would have thought of that myself. I said to this grandfather, "How can you be there as the nephew and I am talking to you here?" He explained to me, "You're limiting yourself again in physical way. This is beyond the physical limitations." The closest I can come to describing it is in the Harry Potter books where the pictures talk. It is a memory of the spirit, and you can actually carry on an intelligent conversation with them. It was kind of like that with the grandfather. It was totally unfamiliar to me, but it taught me a lot.

WHICH SPIRITS COME THROUGH?

Ruth: Why is it that in mediumship readings some people in spirit come through so much more often than others? Someone might find that their sister always comes through, but not their mother?

Neal: Everybody is on a different "speed" of evolution and awareness. Some people who have passed on may not have believed in the possibility of communication in this life, so don't really believe in it or care about it in the afterlife. Others may be so enthralled by everything that is going on in the spirit world that they are not as interested in the physical world. That's just the personality as it evolves its interests. Spirits are sometimes not skilled in coming through, and other times they are.

Story: A husband in spirit who is learning how to come through.

As I was giving mini-messages at the Lily Dale Forest Temple service, I heard in my head, "Ask where Julia is." So I asked if there was somebody in the audience named Julia. She raised her hand. It was her husband who had passed on six months earlier.

Then he put the thought in my head, so I said, "He's leading me to think that you just came from a half-hour reading with a medium and you did not hear from your husband."

She said, "That's right. I had a whole half hour, and he did not come through."

And yet here I am picking him up! Then her husband explained very quickly to me (in thought transference), that he didn't understand how to get through a medium, but now he is learning, through speaking briefly with me, how he can get through. He was excited about that. He said, "Tell her the next time she goes for a reading, I'll know how to do this."

I told her this, and then he told me, "Tell her she has my pants." I'm thinking, "Of course she has your pants, you just died six months ago. She'll have your clothes."

He said, "No. Tell her she has my pants."

Alright. So I just said, "He is telling me to tell you, you have his pants."

She said, "I sure do. I'm wearing them!" Everyone burst out laughing! How evidential for everyone in the audience! If I had censored that, it wouldn't have been as fun. He learned very quickly. He must have guides helping him. He learned how to get through, how to communicate, promised he would come through better next time, and then made a joke. It was so perfect.

WHAT THEY NEED

Ruth: What do the deceased loved ones usually need or want?

Neal: It depends on the person. Some of them need to express their regrets and apologize. Some need to express their continuing love and concern.

They want to express that they are OK and to offer reassurance to the person who is still in the physical. This husband (above) wanted to express that he still loved his wife, he just didn't know how to get through using a medium.

They may still have opinions on the other side, especially if they are just recently passed over.

Sometimes they want to be a cupid, to arrange a relationship for their loved ones. It's as individual as the spirits that are passing over.

Ruth: Are the people in spirit concerned about what is happening here?

Neal: Again, it is not a universal answer. They tend to look at things more from a distance, the perspective of *everything*. Our lives on earth are a flash in the pan. When you are in spirit you realize that life is endless, and the expressions are infinite.

They may be interested in their loved one and the situations they find themselves in, but very rarely will they comment on the political situation. Occasionally they may talk about the possibilities of weather-related incidents or other things like that, but there is more interest in personal things that are going on.

They are interested in relationships, jobs – in so far as the person asks for help. If you don't ask, they may not address that, but if you are interested in it and you want to involve your spirits in it, they'll become interested as well. So in a way, you set the tone about that.

WHEN THERE WAS DISCORD

Ruth: What about when there has been discord with two people and one has crossed over?

Neal: Very often the spirit will come to apologize for the discord. I have never yet had a spirit say, "I was still right," or "I'm glad I did this." They'll come to apologize. If that discord has continued on the spirit side, there is not going to be the communication through a medium.

Many times the person who is getting the reading isn't ready for that, isn't ready to accept the apology or can't handle it.

They'll let it go or say, "I don't want to hear from him," which unfortunately greatly disappoints the spirit who finally made the effort to come through to make amends.

Interesting, one time I had a father come through and apologize to his daughter for some abuse. The daughter said, "He is *always* coming through to apologize, no matter what medium I go to. I am over it!"

But the father wasn't over it, on the spirit side. He had to come through over and over again, just to reaffirm what had already been accepted by the daughter. The *spirit* wasn't satisfied. So it's a two-way street here.

Ruth: So do you think that these rectifications – that come about when there has been discord – benefit those who are in spirit, as well?

Neal: There is no question that these benefit those in spirit as well. They need to express it. When it has been expressed and accepted, there is peace for the spirit, and it eases their further progression in the spirit world.

Ruth: The same way as it does for someone in the physical.

Neal: Yes.

SUICIDES

Ruth: What is your experience with people who have taken their own lives, suicides?

Neal: Again, that varies with the individual. A lot of them have come through and said, "I had no idea how much this would adversely affect everybody else." So they come through to apologize. They were just so involved in their own stuff.

They also come through to assure people that they did not go to hell for that.

Some people who have taken their own lives realize that the conditions under which they did that – either for revenge or depression or whatever – *haven't changed.* After they take their own lives, the conditions are still around them, and they have to work through the problems on the spirit side of life, which may be harder than it would have been in the physical. They often express that they have learned a lot from the suicide.

A few that were called suicides were cries for help on the physical side that were taken too far. They didn't realize that it would *end them.* They wanted to do something dramatic, but it went too far.

Other times, for example with a drug overdose, they'll say, "It wasn't a suicide. I made a mistake and took too much. I didn't realize." So it wasn't really a suicide.

HOW WE CAN COMMUNICATE

Ruth: How can we communicate with a loved one who is in spirit?

Neal: It depends on the individual and their cultural background. If you are Catholic, you can light a candle. The candle symbolizes a light.

When you light a candle here in the physical with an intention of communicating or remembering someone in the spirit realms, it also simultaneously lights a light on the astral or spiritual realms letting that person know they are being thought of.

If you are Native American, you can do prayer ties. Sometimes you can honor them by saving a piece of clothing or a piece of hair. Back in the old days, they used to make pictures out of the hair.

Having a strong thought about the person will bring them in. Often when you do, you will then see a butterfly go by; you'll find a coin on the ground; you'll hear music on the radio that meant something to the two of you.

They don't communicate with, "Hi, how you doing." They communicate with symbols or signs. Sometimes things may even be moved. They will set up certain signals that will reassure you that they are there.

Often when they are needed they will come fairly frequently. But as you get used to it, they will come less frequently because they are not needed as much, and people are evolving in different directions.

VISITING THEIR GRAVES

Ruth: Do they like it when people visit their graves?

Neal: Yes, I have found that to be true. They usually say, "Well you know I am not there, but it is a sweet thing that you do when you visit my grave and you honor me. You put flowers down."

I remember a reading this year. A son came through and said, "You were at my grave in June. Although I am not there, I was there then because I felt your touch and your love. So I came back to that place. But I'm not stuck there."

Those sweet messages come, so I do think doing something like that or lighting a candle with the intention of sending out a thought, "Are you here?" is appreciated.

Visiting a grave definitely amplifies the thought of the person and in an almost physical way connects with a remnant. It's like a loud speaker phone line to the spirit world.

CHILDREN in the SPIRIT WORLD

Neal: Children in the spirit world will come back to a person, through a medium, as the child, but in fact, the child is growing in the spirit world.

They will sometimes come back and say, "Well, you remember me as this child, but I am a grown person in the spirit world." They have their own experiences. They do this phase of their evolution.

They do connect in a loving way to the parents, or the people that knew the child. In some cases, that energy (that person now in spirit) needed to connect on a physical level to then go on to the spirit level to become a guide.

Sometimes they will be like a guardian angel or guide to a person, and they needed the experience of knowing the child in the innocence.

So the children in the spirit world are there and occasionally find it useful to come back and manifest *as the child that was known* and other times come back as a mature person.

*Ruth: I think it's lovely that you bring out that **the child could become a guide for a parent, the sister or brother**, because people may have suspected that.*

ANIMALS in the SPIRIT WORLD

Ruth: What about animals in the spirit world?

Neal: Sometimes a pet will come in with a person [in spirit] that they were connected with. Also, if you had a very strong connection with a dog or a cat, they will come in around you because the love bond is still there. The pets can even almost talk, but they do it in a mental frame. They will even come in with their name sometimes.

Story: Smokey is Here!

Once at an open service at Lily Dale, I was quickly directed to a woman in the back of the audience. All I could see was that she was wearing a chain. I felt the pet, but I wasn't quite sure why. I said, "I am drawn to your chain, and I feel it has a significance with whatever is hanging on it." It was smoky quartz. Then I got, bing!, "Smokey is here." That was the name of her dog. The dog must have been helped by a guide, but the love bond was there. How can a dog give a name? But that was how it worked.

With wild animals, I think they have a group consciousness. So we might get the idea of the energy of a deer or of a grasshopper or something, but the communication isn't there anywhere near like it is with a beloved pet. Those pets are in spirit and they come through. Horses, too!

ADJUSTING to the AFTERLIFE

Ruth: From your perspective is it possible for people who are no longer in their physical bodies to not realize that they have died?

Neal: Especially with sudden deaths, spirits may not realize that they are dead until a few days later. If they are not really connected or spiritually evolved, they can wonder why nobody's paying attention to them anymore. They don't feel any pain or anything. Sooner or later, they realize something is different and they put two and two together. I don't think anybody really gets stuck. They may just stick around for a while, especially if they want to get some message across.

If you look at some of the people who describe their near-death experiences, they don't describe it as being dead. They realize that all of a sudden they are in a different environment. They feel very much alive. Only after they come back into their physical body, do they realize that technically they were dead. But in the meantime, they were having all these lively experiences.

UNINVITED SPIRIT CONTACTS

Ruth: What is your advice to people who have uninvited contact with people in spirit and don't know how to handle it or control it?

First of all, for some people it is exciting. So even though they don't like it, they like it, they want it. So in a subconscious way they are inviting it.

Other times if they do not like it, you can teach them to call their spirit guides in, pray, *ask* for protection, *tell* the spirits, "Don't bother me now." You can direct these people. There's a communication there. Just say, "You're not welcome here." You can also say, "I surround myself with the divine white light of protection. Only that which is the highest and best for my benefit will come through."

If that doesn't feel like enough, you can focus it by doing a little cleansing or *banishing rite* (if you want to call it that). An incantation can focus your consciousness on power and protection. If there is rhythm and rhyme to it, it can be even stronger for you. A good one is:

> *I wash myself with the waters of innocence.*
> *I am cleansed from anything which is not*
> *for my highest and best.*

In the bible there are psalms that carry energy from thousands of years ago. I have modified Psalm 26:6 and use it for myself, my body, my *physical-ness*. Instead of saying, "I wash my *hands* in innocence," I say, "I wash my *self* in innocence." This has a lot of meanings, and I do it in the shower every day.

I wash myself in innocence.
And I go around your altar, Oh Lord,
Listening to your praises and recounting all your
*   wondrous deeds.*
Lord, I love the beauty of your house and the
*   dwelling place of your glory.*
Gather not my soul with those of sinners,
Nor my life with men of blood on whose hands are
*   crimes and whose right hands are full of bribes.*
But as for me, I walk in my integrity.
Redeem me, and have pity on me.
My foot stands on the right path.
In thy assemblies, I will bless the Lord.
Glory be to the Father, and to the Son, and to the
*   Holy Spirit. As it was in the beginning, is now,*
*   and ever shall be. World without end. Amen.*

I do that in the shower every day. It's got power. *The Lord* is my higher self. It is not *God out there.* As I say, "I go around your altar," it's the divine expression, through my soul, coming into the individual.

JUNK CHANNELS

People who are schizophrenic or bipolar sometimes have a natural opening to what I call the *junk channels* of the astral. Spirits are available on all levels of vibration. People who are schizophrenic and bipolar don't necessarily realize when it is physical or nonphysical, nor do they have control over the channel, so they tend to go into the lower channels of the astral – the bothersome channels. If they don't know how to control that with prayer and asking, there are anti-psychotic drugs which basically insulate the vibrations from affecting a person.

NEAL'S FUTURE

Ruth: What do you anticipate happening when you make your own transition into spirit?

Neal: I anticipate meeting certain people that were very formative in my life, like my grandmother, my spiritual teacher, Penny (who is not in spirit yet but will be), and my mom and dad – people I have communicated with here. So I imagine a family reunion.

I imagine continuing to evolve with my spiritual awareness on the other side. I like helping people, so I can imagine myself – maybe part of the time – helping in séances, or being a guide to not any one individual, but maybe to a group – a home circle, or something like that. And I envision enjoying the Is-ness of All as I pass into spirit.

When I was in my twenties, spirit said I would most likely make it to 87. When I was 34, I was diagnosed HIV+. Now in my sixties, it looks like spirit will be correct.

◆◆◆◆◆◆◆◆◆◆◆◆

CHAPTER FIVE

Mediumship

THE LANGUAGE OF MEDIUMSHIP

Story: Learning the "Trick" of Mediumship

During his college years, Neal attended his first spiritual development classes under the tutelage of Rev. Penny Donovan (Thorne) in Albany, NY.

Neal: We would have one hour of class and then one hour of sitting in the dark — total darkness — for psychic development. People would try to give messages and stuff.

I thought it was interesting, but I didn't get any messages. I saw clouds, which was my eyes playing tricks on me, but nothing exciting happened.

The second year the class had dwindled down to about half the original size.

My thought was, "There is really a trick to this. We are learning some nice stuff, but the final thing, where the rubber hits the road, is going to be when they tell us the trick. They are weeding us out to see who is really dedicated, because otherwise, why give us this?"

Ruth: The secret formula!

Neal: In the middle of the second year, we were asked to get up and give messages to people in the third year class. I am thinking, "Nobody told me the trick. How can I do this? They're expecting me to do this!"

So I get up there — not knowing how to do this — and this woman scratches her head. I said, okay, "My attention is drawn to you."

It was hard to explain then, but it's easier to explain now. You know how you can get a book downloaded from the internet in seconds?

So I am looking at her and within seconds I get this memory of driving to Key West nonstop from Albany, NY. We passed through Washington, DC at 3 a.m. The capitol building is there lit up at night.

When the woman scratched her head, the memory of the capitol sort of formed above her head.

Next, I remember seeing my younger brother when he was young playing with little plastic army guys.

So what did that mean to her? I said, "As I am coming into your vibration, I feel that you have Washington on your mind, you must have a son stationed in the army right nearby, and you've been really worried about him."

She said, "Exactly right."

And I thought, "Oh, my God! There's no trick!"

It was totally psychic, but it was an ah-ha experience because the ah-ha experience said, "If there is a trick, it is **learning to trust your imagination and what Spirit suddenly is putting there as a download to make sense to the other person.**"

That was the beginning. I thought, "A year and a half it took me to figure that out!" And from there it became a little easier to do these things.

"So this is how that works!"

That was my second year of spiritual development classes. After a third year I was certified by the church, so I could do little readings in church and stuff.

Ruth: So that first one was a psychic thing. When did you make your first contact with a person in spirit?

Neal: Shortly after that. What I needed was the breakthrough to see how they spoke, which was through your imagination.

So it wasn't very long after that. I would just ask, "Who's around?" and they would tell me.

Ruth: So you weren't seeing it outside of yourself?

Neal: Just in my mind's eye. Like right now, if I say, can you see a Christmas tree? There's no Christmas tree here, but in your mind's eye you know what one looks like. That's how it comes for me. So clairvoyance was my first one.

And you can imagine what *Jingle Bells* sounds like, so that's your clairaudience.

And you have feelings, like why am I being pulled to remember that, so that's the three.

Later I got to learn what symbols mean. At first they were giving me flowers with different colors. Yellow meant education for me, green meant balance.

Ruth: So you developed your own symbolic dictionary? Did you do that overtly or did Spirit give it to you and then you figured it out or...?

Neal: Trial and error. It's still trial and error, 40 years later! *(laughter)*

Penny Donovan (Thorne)

Neal talks about his mentor in mediumship.

Neal: As a medium, Penny was a wonderful role model. She gave wonderful messages that were evidential and people were able to verify. In church she gave short messages, almost everybody would get a message.

Another thing that she did was what I call "Albany-style mediumship." It would start with something like, "I have your grandmother here," and a short identification of spirit. "She is saying _____." Then, "I will leave that with you, have you a question?"

Most people did not want to ask the question out loud, so they would say, "Yes, silent, please." And they would ask it silently. She would say, "Spirit says, _____. Does that make sense?" They would say, "Yes." Then she would move on to the next person.

"Albany-style" Mediumship

1. Short identification of spirit.
2. Short message.
3. Do you have a question? The recipient can ask the question silently.
4. Give spirit's response to the question.
5. Ask if that makes sense to the recipient.

Neal: I think that is a good style of mediumship, and I do it here sometimes. I find it instructive because they ask it silently, which means their spirits listen to the question, their spirits talk to my spirits, and then I give the answer. And if it makes sense, it is like, Wow!

Ruth: So it has more validity to the recipient, because if they asked out loud they would wonder if it is just the medium coming up with an answer.

Neal: Yes. So my spirit team learned how to do that. It was from my modeling after Penny, because that was how she worked.

Giving Everyone an Equal Chance for a Message

Neal: Another thing I do when I chair at the Stump here at Lily Dale is use 3 x 5 cards and have everybody in the audience sign their name. I put the cards all in a basket. The mediums come up and draw three, then give the three people messages.

MEDIUMISTIC or PSYCHIC
An Important Point for Student Mediums

Neal: The first thing I think is important is to know the difference between being psychic with information and being mediumistic. All mediums are psychics, because we can pick up vibrations – which psychics do – but psychics don't emphasize *spirit evidence* of those who have passed on.

Psychics may say, "You're having trouble with your divorce, your job is changing," things like that.

That information *can* come from spirit, as well, but you need to identify the spirits with some evidence like, "Your father is in spirit. His name was Dick. He had a beard, thinning hair." "Yes, that's my dad." "He worked in a factory and then changed to the post office." "Yes, that's my dad." "OK, we have your dad, and *he* is saying you are going through a divorce..."

The psychic picks vibrations (like "you're depressed...") that are basically close to the person, not with the spirits that are around them.

If you are going to be a medium, the first thing you need to start doing is reaching higher than just the person's aura and what is easy to find within that. Instead, reach for what spirits are around.

Not only bring the spirits through, but give evidence that the spirit is really who they say they are, and ideally give evidence that they are still contemporarily aware of what is going on. "Your dad likes what you are doing. He saw you repairing your car two weeks ago and taking care of it the way he used to do." That shows that he is still consciously aware of what you are doing in the *present*, which brings the spirit lovingly to life. It's important that mediums know that.

When I teach "Outdoor Mediumship" in Lily Dale, I emphasize that it is easy to drop down to the psychic level; it's easy to pick up *stuff* around a person. It's harder to pick up spirits. I tell them that spirits have a message, but **reach first to the higher vibration of the spirits**. *Then* let the messages or advice come through. First and foremost, mediumship means bringing through ***evidential* tidbits** on a person's continuance after death (which is what Spiritualism is all about).

FOR THE OUTDOOR MESSAGE SERVICES AT LILY DALE

For public mediumship there are techniques which I teach. One technique is to learn that when you are **talking in front of a large audience,** it is different than when you are giving a one-on-one reading.

First of all, you are looking for **short, concise evidence that spirit is still around**. You want to ideally identify it so that **not only the person** can place it, but that **the audience** can say, "Oh, yes. They are really there."

Then, you want to give **a "greeting,"** not a "reading." Once you identify the spirit and give a little message, don't go on to other spirits for that same person in the audience. **Don't stay with that person**, go on to someone else. Everyone in the audience wants a message, so keep your messages short.

Another thing is to ideally **start in the back** of an audience, because if you start with a person in the front row and start talking to them, you lose the rest of the audience. The energy just drops. You have to be aware of everybody's energy. You need to **bring everyone into it** with some comments that involve the entire audience. You can go to people in the front, but you don't want to start there because you are going to lose the audience.

It's also important to **ask the recipient to verify** the evidence you are giving is accurate. The audience wants to know that. If you read for a person in a low voice or don't ask for clarification, you can be 100% accurate, yet lose the audience. Really, part of it is showmanship.

OUTDOOR MEDIUMSHIP

Ruth: How would you define outdoor mediumship?

Neal: Probably the closest that people might be aware of is *gallery style* mediumship, where you have many people all gathered together. You're not going to be able to reach every one of them, or even a significant minority. You'll just reach a few.

The purpose with everybody gathered together is to demonstrate, using individuals in the audience, that **spirits continue to be conscious and involved in the person's life, and they send love.**

Here at Lily Dale, most of the gallery readings happen outdoors. You get up. You give **three short messages** demonstrating that you are a medium that can connect with spirits, and you have **your own style** – which is interesting, because spirit works differently with everybody, so people are learning that. You are basically educating the whole audience in a gallery style, a group setting.

The audience gets to see a variety of mediums, and we try to get as many messages to the audience as we can. The maximum number of messages that I have seen given at a service of about 200 people is approximately 30. Usually, it is more like 20.

I try to demonstrate both **direct** (client-centered) and **indirect** (spirit-centered) each time I demonstrate. Direct would be, I am going directly to a person in the audience. Indirect would be, "I have somebody (in spirit). Here is what they are saying. Who can place it?"

SPIRIT TEAMS

I asked my spirit team to alternate it like that. I tell my students. "You all have a spirit team that is going to help you, but you can't expect them to do all the work. *You* have to coach *them*. It's a two-way street."

I coached my spirit team by saying, "Look, when I get up there, give me a direct, give me an indirect, give me a little bit of both." If they are not following your coaching, you ask for different spirits. You are allowed to fire your spirits, believe it or not! People often don't realize that.

Don't expect to sit passively and have them spoon feed it to you. They are here to work as a team, but *you* need to set the rules because you're the boss and they are helping you. But they can't help you unless you are specific and say, "Help me with thus and so." I yelled at my spirit team once. I said, "Would you please be more accurate." I'll be giving a message to someone in the back, and the message is really for the person sitting next to them.

Ruth: Is there anything else you would like to say to a student medium?

Neal: Don't ever give up. If you really are truly dedicated, you'll get there. Some faster than others, but you'll get there. Sometimes they look at me up there and I seem so confident and polished. They'll say, "You're so good..." And I say, "Do you know how long it took me to get there? Over forty years." So it doesn't happen overnight.

USE IT OR LOSE IT?

Neal: Some people say, "Use it or lose it," but in my experience, with mediumship and meditation, once you've got it, you don't have to do it every day. It's like riding a bicycle, you can pick up where you left off. It doesn't take long to get back into the swing of it. You might have lost it for a few hours, but not forever.

PHYSICAL MEDIUMSHIP

Ruth: What would you say is the importance and role of having physical mediumship?

Neal: To show that the nonphysical world can influence the physical world. When you see that spirits are able to influence it, by association you should realize that your prayers are able to be heard and acted upon in a physical dimension.

There is an affirmation in my Spiritualist church, The Church of the Living Spirit, "We affirm that communication between all planes of existence is a reality." That is one of our principles.

So physical mediumship shows a communication. They are experimenting with how to communicate with us, and this is one way.

You have mental mediumship where you are showing that your loved ones continue to be conscious on the other side.

Physical mediumship shows that there are *conscious intelligences* that are interdimensional, whether you call them spirits, extraterrestrials, angels...

These intelligences are aware of mankind and can create change around them in the physical world. They show that by lifting people up in the air, creating levitations, using the psychic substance of things to create intelligent messages which are meaningful.

During physical mediumship there is an *interaction* with the spirits speaking to the people in the audience. They may not be people who are family members, but you could call it *interdimensional intelligence* that is speaking to the audience and demonstrating that this interdimensional force can influence.

Ruth: Would you say then that physical evidence is easier for people to accept as real?

Neal: To me that shows there is more than meets the eye. It's a different kind of proof. Certain people need that. Not everyone is built the same way. What makes one person realize that there is more, is different than another.

Some people have the need, like the doubting Thomas (John 20:24-29), "I want to physically feel this."

The medium says, "I see your father standing behind you." You look. There's no Dad standing behind you. When they see it with their physical eyes, like Thomas saw with his physical eyes, that's different.

So I think physical mediumship is needed and it's useful.

Ruth: Do you feel that you needed the physical and were asking for physical proof, or did it just sort of evolve for you?

Neal: You remember that when I had my first reading at age 16 I wanted to know if it was a trick or not. *(see page 6-7)*

I wanted to either prove to myself that there was a spirit world or not.

When you learn about Spiritualism you learn about the old séances. So I learned about physical mediumship and how nobody did it anymore.

Well, why doesn't it happen anymore? The answers given were usually that people don't have enough time to develop, etc. So I thought, I am going to start a group for the purpose of getting physical phenomena. So I started it, and it stopped. I started another one... It's hard to get people to commit to this. We got table tipping, occasionally some rapping, but nothing that was *Wow!*

Can the nonphysical influence the physical?

This became an interest of mine. Okay, now I can do mediumship. Now I have proven to myself there is an existence beyond the physical. Now I want to know, can this existence influence our world in physical ways? Why can't that happen anymore? As a medium, I see in my mind's eye, my clairvoyance, but to see it with my own two physical eyes, I wanted that. Forty years I had been a medium in Lily Dale and other places, and I had yet to see this.

The only time I saw something was in a sweat lodge I once did in Taos, NM, and I thought that was a trick. One of the medicine men brought spirit lights. They were little lights that sparkled all around. I thought maybe he had a lighter with sparkle things on it or something like that.

There were stories about back in the old days in Lily Dale there were precipitated paintings *(they are in the Maplewood Hotel)*. All kinds of stuff. So I thought, "Well, where is it? Why isn't it happening now?" I knew that *like attracts like*.

So if I wanted to do it, I needed to be where people were already doing it.

Neal went on to tell about going to France, England, and Spain where he did witness physical phenomena with mediums.

Neal: After that I was back in Lily Dale at a home circle, not completely dark, just curtains drawn. We were doing some table tipping, but that can be done with psychokinetic energy. Spirit can manipulate that *type* of energy, but table tipping doesn't necessarily show the presence of spirit.

Since then we have gotten the table to completely levitate off the ground and even walk on the ceiling. I said, "I am not going to believe it until I see it completely levitate off the ground." I had seen it done by someone else, so I knew it could be done.

So I am at this little home circle, we did a little table tipping, but then when we were just sitting there, the trumpet went sliding right across the table all by itself!

I thought, "I had to go to France, England, and Spain to see this, and *now* I see it in Lily Dale. Finally! Because like attracts like, and now I had opened up that doorway.

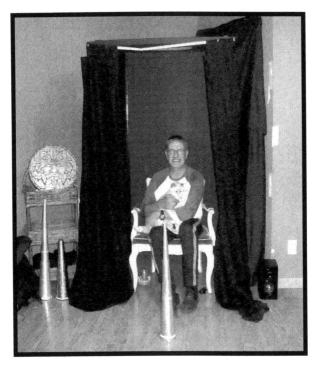

Neal and his cat sit in the cabinet in his séance room.

Now I have a regular group that has been sitting for about seven years, every Thursday night. That is finally how we got the table to go up, because it takes that long to get all this energy together. We are hoping for more, so we continue to sit. I have also invited mediums from abroad to my séance room.

You can fake some of this stuff if people don't know any better, and they are in complete darkness. If you see a trumpet float in front you, it looks like spirit is doing that, but a person could be doing that. So it is easy to wonder, "Are they faking it or not," if you are in the dark. Yet genuine "physical phenomena" does happen, and sometimes complete darkness is needed for it to manifest.

———————

Neal now offers the following workshops at the Lily Dale Assembly, Lily Dale, NY:

- "Outdoor Mediumship in Lily Dale"
- "Health & Healing with Alternative Therapies"
- "Edgar Cayce Remedies"
- "Holistic Nutrition from Edgar Cayce and Others"

♦♦♦♦♦♦♦♦♦♦♦♦♦

CHAPTER SIX

A Doctor
and a Medium

Story: A Remedy from Spirit

Neal: Noralee was one of my patients who had AIDS. She had cryptosporidiosis diarrhea, and back in the 1990's there was no cure for that. They would just have horrendous diarrhea and it was hard to control, even with tincture of opium and all these things. Previous to her, I had a person completely cure himself of cryptosporidiosis diarrhea by using castor oil packs (which is an Edgar Cayce remedy), and he lived for a couple of years more before he died of other AIDS-related things. I knew the castor oil packs didn't work for everybody. I tried it on her and it didn't work. So I needed something to control the diarrhea.

So I tuned into spirit. *Tincture of walnut* is what I came up with. I happened to have some that I made myself. You put green hulls from black walnut in a jar with 100% proof vodka and let it sit. It becomes a black liquid. So I gave her some of that.

One quarter teaspoon a day was all she needed to control her diarrhea, so she was comfortable. So that taught me to listen to spirit for help, and that we can do what Edgar Cayce did, too.

As things progressed, she knew it was time coming up (that she would pass on) so she made me a wall hanging for helping her in her last years. So I think of her when I am in my kitchen and I see it.

EDGAR CAYCE

Neal: As a third year resident in family practice, they allowed us to have a month elective, whatever we wanted to do, so I went to Phoenix, Arizona and spent a month at the A.R.E. Clinic (Edgar Cayce Association for Research and Enlightenment). Drs. Bill and Gladys McGarey, the physicians there, used Edgar Cayce principles.

See thefoundationforlivingmedicine.org for more about Dr. Gladys Taylor McGarey, MD, MD(H).

I knew that in medical school I would learn a lot about physical, scientific medicine. But I also knew, having spiritually developed and read Edgar Cayce, that there is more to the physical body and medicine than just physical things. There is a spiritual element. There is an emotional element. There is a mental element

As a matter of fact, in medical school we were taught that when a female patient is very sick, *nigh unto death*, one of the first signs that she is going to make it and do better is that she has her make up on when you come into the room. It's not in the medical text books, but you see this. So you know it is mind, body, spirit. I see that time and again.

TO ALL PHYSICIANS:
- **We are more than the physical body.**
- **Connect the dots.**

You asked what I would like to tell other physicians. One thing I would like to say is, "Don't forget that we are more than the physical body. We have emotions that influence our disease. We have a family structure and communities that are influencing our whole way of thinking."

All of it filters into the state of health that an individual finds themselves in. It is a *holistic* viewpoint that you have to take, even if your specialty is cardiology – there is more than just that. There is *heartbreak*, which is often associated with heart attacks. The heart attack often comes about six months later. Very interesting: **the lag between an emotional or spiritual crisis and the physical manifestation takes about 6-9 months.** So when you see something in the physical, look back 6-9 months earlier, and often you will see a precipitating event.

In the cardiac unit I would talk to the heart attack patients and a lot of times they had lost their son, or had some other heartbreak, about nine months before the heart attack. It's something you don't think about or connect the dots with right away. If it happened last week, it would be easier.

So if I could tell all the physicians something, I would say, "Connect the dots." When you look for that 6-9 month precipitating event, you find it. That's one example of the mind-body-spirit connection that is definitely there.

CASTOR OIL

At the Cayce clinic, as well as learning about the mind-body-spirit connection, I learned about the benefits of castor oil (externally). Cayce talked about castor oil packs. I have used it with great success in treating resistant fungal infections, allergies, skin eczema. Castor oil is cheap and easy to use for a lot of different things. It's one of the Cayce remedies that I have expanded from what he recommended and have had great results with patients that use it.

I learned a lot of Cayce principles that I teach in my workshops. They are still as useful today as they were when Cayce gave them in the early part of the 20th century. There is always something new coming out in the medical journals, but his stuff has been consistent right along.

COMBINING SPIRITUAL WISDOM WITH MEDICINE

Neal: You come into this earth and have experiences, "You're not good enough; you'll never amount to anything." All this negativity, which we as kids believe and carry with us.

One of the big lessons is self-acceptance, "God doesn't make no junk." God didn't make you to be a piece of junk and be worthless. There is a value to you and the way you think.

For me, God didn't make me *gay* as a condemnation, to "send you to hell." He gave it as "an opportunity to unfold your awareness and understanding of people, so use it in a positive way."

Life's teaching is to look for the good and praise it (as the bumper sticker says), and *you make your world the way you think.*

When I see gay people, or anybody with anything that makes them feel uncomfortable or less than they really are, I try to make it easy and take the stigma out of it and make it feel like, "This is alright."

Being an HIV doctor, the people that have stigma, chips on their shoulders, anger about how they are, what they thought, what they did, those are the people who are no longer around today to tell me about it. They died.

But the people that changed their life and changed their mind — I've learned this from so many stories — thrived. Maybe they died, but they died in a better state of mind than they would have otherwise.

Story: "Your attitude is going to kill you."

Neal: Dennis was a patient in the AIDS clinic before we had good meds. He'd come in with a chip on his shoulder. "You guys don't understand nothin'. This is a plot by the government to kill off the gay people. You can't take my blood pressure!" He was always angry. Nothing was right.

The nurses would come to me and say, "Dennis is here. *You* take his blood pressure and put him in a room." It was that bad.

So I'd go in and I'd say, "Dennis, I'm in the same boat you are. I am HIV+, too." He didn't believe it, until the nurses verified it to him. "But I'm doing well, and you're not."

Every time I saw him I would say, "Dennis, the reason you are not doing well is because you have a lousy attitude."

"No, I don't…"

I kept telling him, as gently as I could, "Your attitude is going to kill you. It will send you to your grave fast."

Finally, he came in in a wheelchair with oxygen, and he had what we call *the look*—sunken eyes, vacant stare. It means you're going to die within the next two weeks.

I said, "Dennis, you have *the look*."
He looks at me and goes, "What's *the look*?"

I was trying to be nice to him. I said, "It means you're going to be dead within a month."

"A month, huh?"
"Yea."
"Can I go on a cruise?"

What am I going to say? With his oxygen and his wheelchair... I said, "Well, do you have someone to wheel you onto the cruise and help you with your oxygen tank?"

"Yea, I have a guy who'll go with me."
"Go. But do it within the next week. Can you do that?"
"Yes."

I am thinking, "I'm sending a dead man on a ship. They're going to call me. What am I doing!"

Three weeks pass by, and Dennis comes into the office. And he doesn't have *the look* anymore. I said, "How was your cruise?"

He says, "I have one week left, right?" (because I had told him a month).

"Yea…"

"With the time I had left, it didn't make any sense to be mad at anybody, do anything, get in anybody's way, so I said, 'Oh, f--- it. I'm just going to have a good time on the cruise.' So I really enjoyed myself."

That was a turning point. He got better. He gained weight. He gained energy, threw away the oxygen tank, and for two and a half years, was a different Dennis.

He formed a block club because he was interested in other people and getting them together. He brought me over for supper about a year after all of this. He said, "You know, you told me for years it was my attitude. I didn't believe you. But then I changed it on that cruise, and that was the best thing that happened to me."

He was a smoker and he died of cryptococcal meningitis about two and a half years later. But he died quickly and the attitude change gave him two and a half years of good life. There was still no cure for AIDS back when he died, but he still had a good life.

◆◆◆◆◆◆◆◆◆◆◆◆◆

CHAPTER SEVEN

Philosophies
and Beliefs

Ruth: Do you believe in God?

Neal: Yes. God has many names, whether it is God, Allah, Buddha, Nirvana, All That Is, Infinite Intelligence... I think God is much more than we can understand. God is, in fact, infinite. God is everything, and we have not even scratched the surface on what we think "Everything" is. God is everything, and everything is much more than we have any clue of.

A look at Neal's car shows us some of his beliefs.

Ruth: Does God have a plan?

Neal: I don't know enough about the huge Is-ness of God to know if there is a plan for God. If there is a plan, it is way beyond my understanding.

Ruth: If you could help everyone in the world understand something, what would that be?

Neal: Understand that you are a small part of who you really are, manifesting here in this earth, and that nothing lasts forever, as far as you as an individual goes. You will surely merge with the God, Is-ness, All That Is, eventually. Although, when we are caught in the midst of our crises we think that's the only thing. We need to broaden our horizon.

Ruth: What is it that you think throws people off their path?

Neal: There are several things. One of them is expectations. We create expectations and when they are not met, we are thrown for a loop and are thrown off our path. When we "Let go and let God," so to speak – which means that our expectations are possibilities that we don't hold a lot of emotional stuff with – the flow goes smoother. What throws people off the path is resisting going with the flow; they resist change. Whenever you have expectations, it is a setup for disappointment.

Ruth: Why do you think we come into this life, and what is the purpose of living this life?

Neal: I think it is a different answer for everybody. I remember when I was four or five. My mother was having a particularly hard day, and I began thinking, "Why am I here? And why are all these people here? Is there really a God? And if there is a God, why did God send us here? All these troubles people are having...

"Well, whether there is a God or not, they are having enough trouble, so I think during my life the least I could do is not cause *more* trouble for them. Just try to stay out of their way."

That was my thinking as a five year old, and that has sort of stuck with me. People have enough stuff. If you can't help them, just stay out of their way.

So I didn't know why I was there, but if I *was* there, people were having enough trouble, and that if I could help in some way that would be good whether there was a God or not.

If in the end there was a heaven, that would just be an extra plus. If there wasn't, at least I did some good by staying out of people's way and trying to do the best I could while I was here.

Ruth: Is that what you still basically believe?

Neal: It sticks with me to this day, but it expanded from there. The basic underlying premise is probably still the same, but now I *know* there is a spirit world that is far greater than just "Here we are on earth. There we are in heaven." No. Many, many layers, "many, many mansions" (John 14:2).

We're just scratching the surface down here, and there are many worlds that are not God, they are not heaven, but they are a step up from where we are at. And we continue to evolve.

So we're down on this earth with a soul which probably is experiencing many lifetimes together (because there is no time in the spirit world). And we are trying this out and trying that out, and we are blending with *all that is*, because we are — you are me, I am you, we are all part of God, so we all are joined — and God is discovering him/herself by expressing in all these different ways.

So I am an expression of God experimenting. But other expressions of God, I don't want to hinder them, so I'll stay out of their way. Let them have their own path, let them do their own thing.

Judge not, lest you be judged
because in what manner ye judge,
it is judged back to you.
Matthew 7:1

There are lessons in my life that I came here to learn (for me, anger and impatience), but in learning them I try to make it as easy as I can on everybody else and to understand that they have their own problems. If I can reach out and help them with their problems, I think I have helped both of us.

With people who are searching, if I can show them what brings me joy... We can help people by radiating it, by teaching, by looking for the good in them and choosing it.

Story: "I love you."

Neal: Bruce and his partner, Tom, were friends of mine. I shared some of my spiritual beliefs with them, and Bruce was kind of interested in that. When I described a spirit I was aware of in their house, Bruce said, "That fits what I thought I saw." So he had a sensitivity for spirit and started to read spiritual books.

One day he told me, "You know, people who don't know about spiritual presences can't choose the time of their death, so they usually die in the middle of the night," (most people do die in the middle of the night).

So Bruce says, "So I'm going to die at high noon. That's what I'm going to do."

The other thing he told me was he felt he was not good enough. He never ever heard his mother say, "I love you."

There was always this unspoken message that you are not good enough because you do not give me kids (grandchildren) and this gay stuff. So he had this guilt, Jewish guilt, that he carried around with him.

He wanted to confront his mother with this. He had a psychologist that he was working with over these issues, hoping that would help him heal (he had AIDS). He was also on a macrobiotic diet, and was one of the first patients that I put on AZT when it first came out.

I went out of town for a few days, but as I was there eating lunch I had the impulse to call Bruce and see how he was doing. His partner answered the phone. "It's funny you called. Bruce just died a minute ago."

Then Tom told me the story of what had happened. One of the things Bruce wanted to do to complete his life was to confront his mother (about never telling him she loved him). He actually got the psychologist to make a home visit the evening before he died.

Bruce had been going in and out of coma, but with the psychologist and his parents there, Bruce turned to his parents and said, "I have never heard you say, 'I love you.'"

Then as his parents were saying, "What do you mean we never said that? Look at all the things we did for you… ?" he slipped into his final coma.

They never said it, but he got that off his chest. He died peacefully at noon the next day (just as he had said he would). He "healed into death."

———————

My father loved me. He helped me build this house. But he was not the kind to say, "I love you." Until one time, when he found out I was HIV positive (it was a while after that, but he got to thinking) and it is something I treasure.

He said, "I don't understand how you are, and I tolerate your friends, but you are my son and I love you anyway." That one sentence stays with me forever. It was beautiful.

Ruth: The potential and the power of what something like that can mean to someone. How important it is to do that.

Neal: Yes, I treasure that one time. And it was enough for his entire life. It was wonderful. What a gift. And I thought of Bruce, thinking of what a gift I got.

Ruth: What experience would you wish for each person in the world?

Neal: To know that they mattered, and they are loved. If you are loved, then you matter. That would give a lot of peace to the world.

If no matter what *other* people think, say, do, or love, if people knew they were loved and they mattered, then we could get rid of the religious wars, all these opinions, and all that stuff. It would be a better place.

✦✦✦✦✦✦✦✦✦✦✦✦✦✦

You matter.

You are loved.

✦✦✦✦✦✦✦✦✦✦✦✦✦✦

Neal's Recommended Reading List

SPIRITUALITY & WISDOM

Dhammapada: The Sayings of the Buddha

Translation: Thomas Byrom, 1976

Neal: My absolute favorite sacred scriptural passage is chapter one of the rendering of the Dhammapada by Thomas Byrom. The name of the chapter in most renderings is *Twins*, but Byrom names it *Choices*. It is the most important chapter of sacred literature because it shows why our thought influences and creates our world. Nothing is more important than the choice of thought that you make. Understanding your power of choice and how you create your own world. This summarizes my modus operandi in life.

In Tune with the Infinite* or Fullness of Peace, Power, and Plenty

Authors: Ralph Waldo Trine, 1866

Neal: The preface says it all and it echoes what the Dhammapada says. "The optimist is right. The pessimist is right." Then it says the difference between the two depends on the choice you make.

*Note: A free Kindle eBook edition is available.

Practical Occultism in Daily Life

Author: Dion Fortune, 1981

Neal: The most useful chapters in this book are 2 and 3, *Control of the Environment*. How to deal with your fear. How to live life to the fullest. The power of choice is echoed in there in that you have the choice to influence your environment, rather than letting the environment dictate how you should feel. You can overcome that. If you are in an area where there are a lot of depressed people, you tend to get depressed because of entrainment with that vibration. You can overcome that by changing the vibration. So it shows you your power, the power that you can use.

The Aquarian Gospel of Jesus the Christ

Author: Levi H. Dowling, 1908, 1969

The Bible

Especially the Book of Deuteronomy, 30: 11 onward.

Energy Anatomy: The Science of Co-Creation and Your Power of Choice

Author: Caroline Myss, PhD., 1999

Neal recommends this for the insights it brings regarding health and well-being. There are energy drains that you carry around through your chakras. It helps you realize what's happening and then how to get insights into how to improve that "drain." He prefers the audio version of her lecturing, rather than the book.

PSYCHIC DEVELOPMENT

You Can Change Your Life Through Psychic Power

Author: Jo Anne Chase as told to Constance Moon, 1960

Neal: This is for developing your psychic awareness and those interested in mediumship. Especially useful for people who are just starting out. Neal uses this when he teaches.

NATIVE AMERICAN, LAKOTA

Mother Earth Spirituality: Native American Paths to Healing Ourselves and Our World

Author: Ed McGaa, 1990

Neal recommends this as a good introduction into Native American thinking and spirituality. The author is part Lakota, part Scottish.

HEALTH & HEALING

The Edgar Cayce Handbook Through Drugless Therapy

Author: Dr. Harold J. Reilly, 1981

Neal: If you are interested in alternative or complementary medicine and useful, practical applications of it, this is an excellent book. Diet, skin problems, exercises, the benefits of castor oil. Interesting things, and useful if you try them.

The Relaxation Response
Author: Herbert Benson, M.D.
First published in 1975
Neal: A simple method to ease stress and relax the mind. A result of research done at Harvard University. Instead of using classic mantras, a person can simply repeat the word, "one."

TEACHING STORY

Illusions: The Adventures of a Reluctant Messiah
Author: Richard Bach, 1978
Neal: It teaches us about the illusions we operate under which are not necessarily true, and yet our world is sometimes governed by them. It's a great book to shake you out of the way you are habitually thinking and open yourself to something more spiritual, on a practical level.

FOR FUN

Harry Potter Book Series
Author: J.K. Rowling, 1997-
Neal recommends these as an escape that carries a message of love. They give you a sense of wonderment and magic in the world, the sense of push-pull good-evil balance. Harry Potter wasn't necessarily an angel. They show you how life happens, all kinds of things can happen and you can get benefits out of it. It's a wonderful way to relax.

Recommended Newsletter

Inner Whispers: A Free Spiritual Newsletter by VERONICA

April Crawford, trance medium

www.aprilcrawford.com

Neal: There is a monthly newsletter as well as YouTube videos. She speaks about her philosophy that we are living in the linear and don't see things from the eternal, very simple philosophy. She also answers questions from people.

Online Physical Mediumship Community

physicalmediumship4u.ning.com

Neal's Website

nealrzepkowski.com, docnealmedium.com

Neal on Facebook

facebook.com/neal.rzepkowski

Additional Resources

from Ruth Shilling

Lily Dale Assembly
Lily Dale, NY 14752 USA   (716) 595-8721
lilydaleassembly.com
The world's largest center for the science,
philosophy and religion of Spiritualism. Classes and
activities are mostly offered during the summer
months. There are 50+ registered mediums who
live and serve there in the daily services.

Arthur Findlay College
Stansted, UK   arthurfindlaycollege.org
01279 81 3636, 00 44 127 981 3636
A residential facility where students study spiritual
and psychic enfoldment, Spiritualist philosophy,
Spiritualist healing, and kindred disciplines.
Considered to be the foremost school for Evidential
Mediumship in the world.

The Journey Within Church
25 Carr St., Pompton Lakes, NJ 07442 USA
(973) 616-9685   journeywithin.org
The pastor, Rev. Janet Nohavec, is a tutor at Arthur
Findlay College and hosts a full schedule of tutors
from the AFC at her church in New Jersey, USA.

The Inner Quest Foundation

AFC Tutors Brian Robertson and Simon James
Victoria, BC V8W 2R9 Canada
1-250-383-1012   innerquestfoundation.com
An educational center devoted to the ethical and
spiritual development of those wishing to pursue
the Intuitive Arts.

Fellowships of the Spirit

282 Dale Drive, Lily Dale, NY 14752 USA
(716) 595-2159   www.fellowshipsspirit.org
Both introductory and in-depth training in multiple
disciplines — mediumship, healing arts & spiritual
studies.

Forever Family Foundation

222 Atlantic Avenue, Oceanside, New York 11572
(631) 425-7707
www.foreverfamilyfoundation.org
Goal: To further the understanding of Afterlife
Science through research and education while
providing support and healing for people in grief.
Events, discussion groups, medium panel, visionary
explorers group, Signs of Life Radio, Signs of Life
magazine, and more.

Online Resources:

SNUi : Spiritualists' National Union International Evidential Mediumship Online Learning.
www.snui.org
Mediumship classes, and practice with others worldwide.

Gaia, formerly Gaiam TV.
www.gaia.com (not www.gaiaonline.com)
An online subscription service similar to Netflix but specializing in metaphysical topics, spirituality, personal growth, yoga, mysticism, health, psychic phenomena... There are a multitude of excellent interviews with leading thought leaders, authors and teachers, as well as short and full length films, including *Astral City* (or *Our Home*), the Spiritist classic from a book by Chico Xavier.

YouTube Channel:

After Life TV with Bob Olson
youtube.com/user/AfterlifeTVChannel
There are many interesting videos with Bob Olson interviewing mediums, psychics, and people who have contributed to the field of spiritual development.

About the Author

 **Ruth Shilling**, M.M. (Viola Performance), has had a rich and varied career. Beginning as a professional musician — both in Germany and the USA — she later became involved in healing using Therapeutic Touch, sound healing and other subtle energy techniques. The classes she taught in those modalities later moved into an emphasis on spiritual growth and the ability to hear and know the guidance of the Spirit.

While on a second visit to Egypt (1998), she sat in meditation at the Luxor Temple and was asked by the spirits of the place to "bring the people that we may work with them directly."

What she understood from that request was that the metaphysical and spiritual tours being offered were basically using Egypt as a backdrop for the teachings of the guest speakers on those tours. What the spirits of the place wanted was to work directly with the spiritual seekers who came to the temples. They even suggested an itinerary that would enable this!

Ruth answered the call and created the ***All One World Egypt Tours*** company. More than 50 tours have resulted from this alliance, and the spirits of the place have taught many, including Ruth herself, during those encounters.

Another tap on the shoulder from Spirit came with an idea of how to help people manifest more of what they want in life by using the easy, free and childlike state that comes about when we are coloring designs. This resulted in the *"**Color It True**" **Adult Coloring Books*** series. Each of these is a collection of mandala designs with embedded symbolism for facilitating manifestation, powering up affirmations, or sending positive energies and prayers to those we love. The open space in the center of each design creates a place to focus the intent of the person who is coloring the designs.

The inspiration for the ***Through a Medium's Eyes*** series of books is described in the introduction. Hopefully the ideas, experiences and stories in these books will inspire you to clarify and enlarge your own visions and perspectives on life.

See Ruth's current activities on Facebook and at:
- all1world.com
- spiritualmedium1.com

Contact: a1w.books@gmail.com

Produced by Ruth Shilling

The Ancient Egyptian Gods & Goddesses Cards

A set of colorful cards to use as inspiration or a tool to connect with the "saints" of Ancient Egypt.

Available through: godsgoddessescards.com

or all1world.com

Additional Books by Ruth Shilling

Through a Medium's Eyes Series

About Life, Love, Mediumship, and the Spirit World

Rev. B. Anne Gehman, Volume 1

Carol Gasber, Volume 2

Neal Rzepkowski, M.D., Volume 3

Rev. Simon James, Volume 4

Rev. Brian Robertson, Volume 5

Color It True: *Adult Coloring Books that Draw Good Things to You!*

Marvelous Manifestation Mandalas

Magnetic Manifestation Mandalas

Miraculous Manifestation Mandalas

Angelic Manifestation Mandalas

Abundance Manifestation Mandalas

SUCCESS with the Violin and Life:
Strategies, Techniques and Tips for Learning Quickly and Doing Well. See successviolin.com.

SINAI: *The Desert & Bedouins of South Sinai's Central Regions.* Palm Press, Cairo, Egypt, 2004 Contains more than 100 full-color photos of the Sinai and the Bedouin people who live there.

♦♦♦♦♦♦♦♦♦♦♦♦♦

Made in the USA
Middletown, DE
01 February 2019